SPACE STATIONS

ABDO
Publishing Company

A Buddy Book **by Marcia Zappa**

Buddy **BOOKS**
The Universe

VISIT US AT
www.abdopublishing.com

Published by ABDO Publishing Company, 8000 West 78th Street, Edina, Minnesota 55439.

Printed in the United States of America, North Mankato, Minnesota.
102010
012011

 PRINTED ON RECYCLED PAPER

Coordinating Series Editor: Rochelle Baltzer
Contributing Editors: Megan M. Gunderson, BreAnn Rumsch, Sarah Tieck
Graphic Design: Maria Hosley
Cover Photograph: *NASA*.
Interior Photographs/Illustrations: *AP Photo*: Mikhail Metzel (p. 29), NASA-HO, File (p. 28); *NASA*: Sandra Joseph, Kevin O'Connell (p. 13), JSC June 2, 2008 (p. 9), JSC June 9, 2008 (p. 16), JSC June 10, 2008 (p. 11), NASA (pp. 5, 7, 9, 15, 17, 19, 20, 21, 23, 25, 26, 27, 29); *Photo Researchers, Inc.*: Ria Novosti (p. 24), Victor Habbick Visions (p. 30).

Library of Congress Cataloging-in-Publication Data

Zappa, Marcia, 1985-
  Space stations / Marcia Zappa.
     p. cm. -- (The universe)
  ISBN 978-1-61714-693-0
  1. Space stations--Juvenile literature. I. Title.
  TL797.15.Z37 2011
  629.44'2--dc22
                              2010037086

Table Of Contents

What Is a Space Station?

People have observed objects in the night sky for thousands of years. At first, they could only study space from the ground.

In the 1950s, people began sending spacecraft to **explore** space. Soon after, **astronauts** started traveling to space!

As space travel increased, scientists created space stations. **Astronauts** can live and work in space stations for long periods of time.

Since 1971, scientists have launched nine successful space stations.

A Closer Look

Space stations **orbit** Earth. They are larger than other spacecraft. This gives **astronauts** more room to live and work.

Space stations have many uses. Astronauts use them to observe space and do science experiments. They also use them to store supplies for space **missions**.

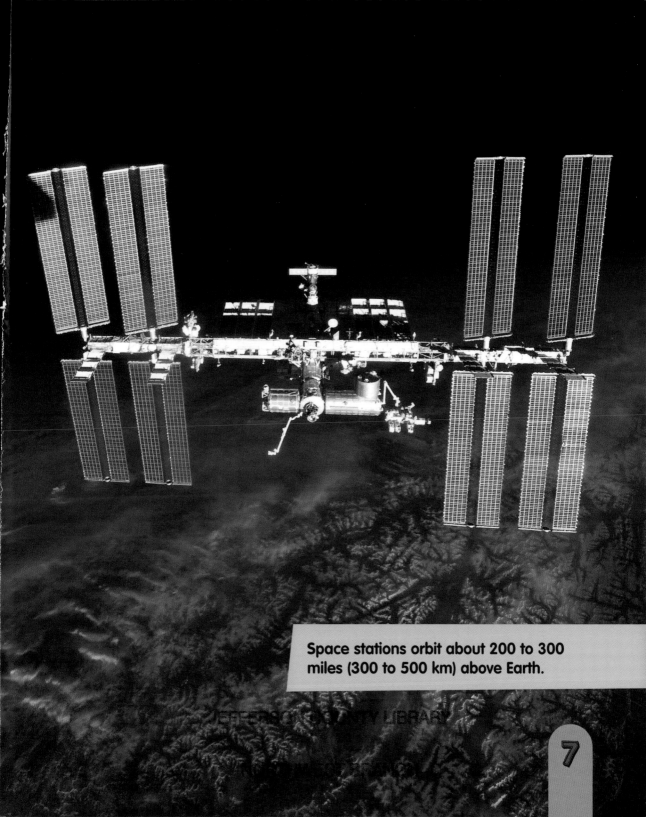

Space stations orbit about 200 to 300 miles (300 to 500 km) above Earth.

7

Getting to Space

Powerful engines called rockets **launch** space stations. Today's space stations are very large. So, they are sent to space in sections. Then, **astronauts** put the parts together in space.

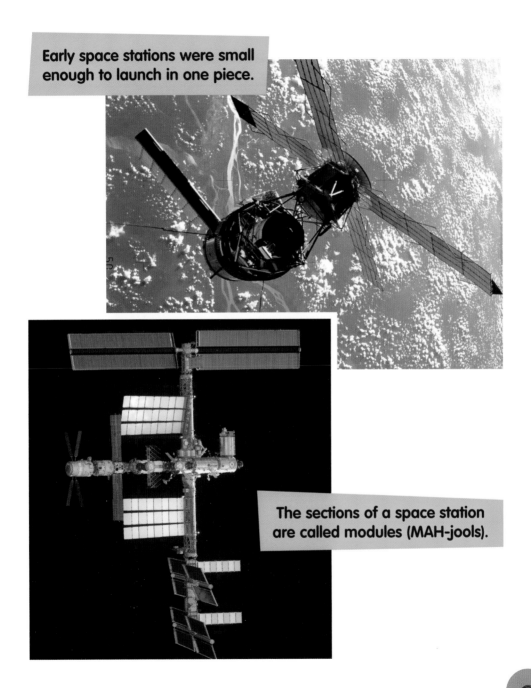

Early space stations were small enough to launch in one piece.

The sections of a space station are called modules (MAH-jools).

Building space stations is slow, hard work. Often, **astronauts** continue to work on them after they are built. They may add new sections or tools. And, they fix or replace parts as they wear out.

Solar panels turn sunlight into power for a space station. If a panel breaks, astronauts fix or replace it.

There and Back

Spacecraft such as shuttles bring **astronauts** and supplies to and from space stations. Astronauts living at a space station are called crew members. A crew spends about 100 to 200 days at a space station.

Spacecraft called probes carry supplies to space stations. They fly without people. Probes bring water, food, and tools. They also carry mail to crew members.

Rockets launch space shuttles (*above*) and space probes.

When a spacecraft reaches a space station, it **docks** with it. A spacecraft connects to a station at a docking port.

Spacecraft and space stations have special doors called hatches. At a docking port, a spacecraft lines up its hatch with the space station's. Then, the hatches are opened. This creates a tunnel that connects them.

Docking a spacecraft with a space station
is called a rendezvous (RAHN-dih-voo).

Space Travel

Conditions in space are very different than on Earth. The force of **gravity** is less noticeable in an **orbiting** space station. This makes **astronauts** float around as if they are weightless!

Many astronauts sleep in sleeping bags. They strap themselves to a surface so they don't float away!

Astronauts regularly check on a space station's systems. If they are not working properly, crew members must fix them.

It can feel very hot or very cold in space. So, a space station has a system that keeps the temperature at the right level.

In space, there is nearly no air. So, space stations have air tanks. Fans send out fresh air to the crew. Filters take in used air.

Sometimes, **astronauts** work outside a space station. Out in space, they wear space suits. These special suits **protect** them from heat and cold. They also guard them from being hit by small space objects.

Space suits allow astronauts to survive in space for about seven hours. They have everything an astronaut needs including air, water, and tools to remove waste.

A radio inside a space suit lets an astronaut talk to crew members.

Important Work

Astronauts at a space station work five to six days a week. Most of their work is related to science.

Astronauts study Earth and its atmosphere. They also observe the sun, the moon, the planets, and the stars. And, they do science experiments.

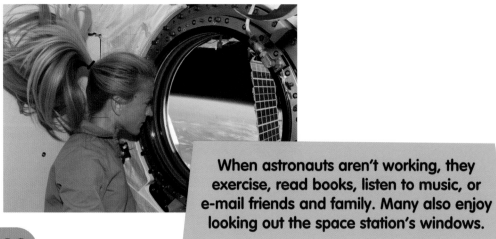

When astronauts aren't working, they exercise, read books, listen to music, or e-mail friends and family. Many also enjoy looking out the space station's windows.

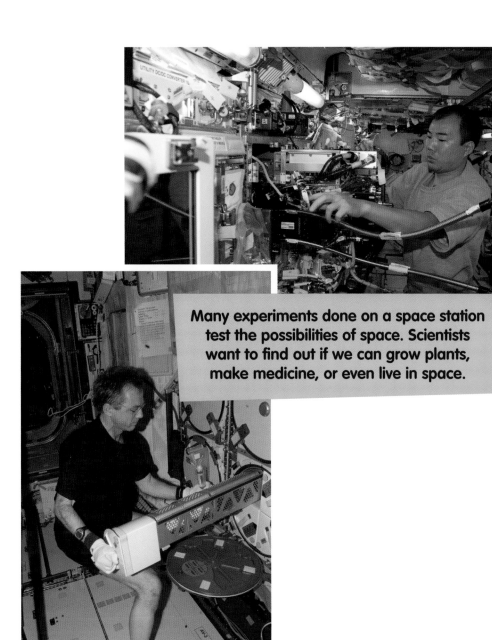

Many experiments done on a space station test the possibilities of space. Scientists want to find out if we can grow plants, make medicine, or even live in space.

Early Space Stations

The first space station was **launched** by the Soviet Union in 1971. It was called Salyut 1. In 1973, the United States sent Skylab into **orbit**. These stations held supplies to support **astronauts** for many months.

From 1973 to 1974, three crews visited Skylab. They did almost 300 science experiments.

Valery Polyakov was a Mir astronaut. From 1994 to 1995, he lived in space for almost 438 days in a row. This set a record!

In 1986, the Soviet Union **launched** a more advanced space station. It was called Mir. Mir had several sections. Crews of **astronauts** took turns living and working in it.

By 2001, Mir started to wear out. So, scientists allowed it to fall from **orbit**. Most of Mir burned up as it entered Earth's **atmosphere**. What was left fell into the ocean.

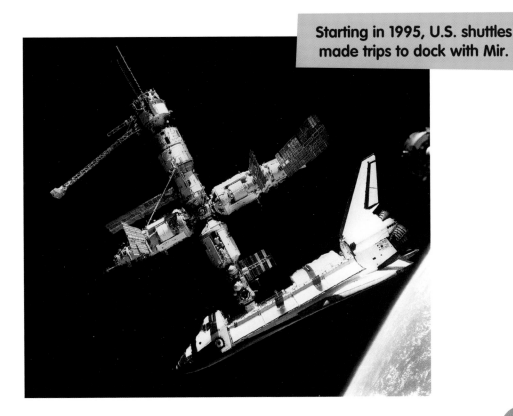

Starting in 1995, U.S. shuttles made trips to dock with Mir.

The ISS

In 1998, scientists from around the world started building a large space station. It is called the International Space Station (ISS). Three **astronauts** moved into the ISS in 2000. Today, the ISS has six crew members.

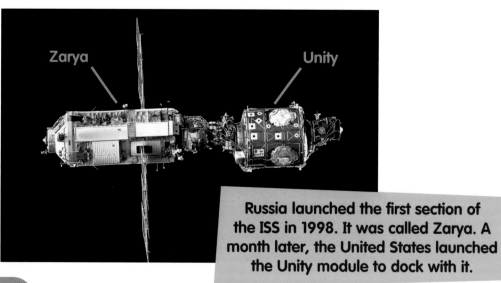

Zarya

Unity

Russia launched the first section of the ISS in 1998. It was called Zarya. A month later, the United States launched the Unity module to dock with it.

The ISS is about the size of a five-bedroom home. It orbits Earth about 16 times a day.

Scientists expect to complete the ISS in 2011. By then, more than 80 spacecraft flights will have been made to it. And, the completed ISS will have eight large sections.

Fact Trek

In space, **astronauts** use salt and pepper in liquid form. If they were solids, like on Earth, they would float off the food!

Exercise is important for astronauts at a space station. They work out for about two hours each day. Many astronauts run on treadmills. Special cords keep them from floating away!

In 2007, astronaut Sunita Williams ran a marathon on a space station treadmill! A marathon is 26.2 miles (42.2 km) long.

In 2001, the first space **tourist** traveled to the ISS. Space tourists are not working **astronauts**. They pay money to travel to space for fun.

Dennis Tito was the first space tourist. He spent six days at the ISS.

Space stations are built like buildings on Earth with floors, walls, windows, and ceilings. This helps astronauts know which way is up! It keeps them from feeling dizzy, lost, or confused in space.

Voyage to Tomorrow

The ISS continues to be important for working in space. It was built to last for about 15 years. But by fixing and replacing old parts, it could last longer.

Scientists have plans to build new space stations. Someday, they hope to build a space station on the moon!

Artists and scientists imagine what a space station on the moon would look like.

Important Words

astronaut a person who is trained for space travel.

atmosphere (AT-muh-sfihr) the layer of gases that surrounds a space object.

dock to join two spacecraft while in space.

explore to go into in order to make a discovery or to have an adventure.

gravity a natural force that pulls toward the center of a space object. It also pulls space objects toward each other.

launch to send off with force.

mission the sending of spacecraft to do certain jobs.

orbit the path of a space object as it moves around another space object. To orbit is to follow this path.

protect (pruh-TEHKT) to guard against harm or danger.

tourist a person who travels for pleasure.

Web Sites

To learn more about **space stations**, visit ABDO Publishing Company online. Web sites about **space stations** are featured on our Book Links page. These links are routinely monitored and updated to provide the most current information available.

www.abdopublishing.com

INDEX